TIME
FOR KIDS

Technology
Feats & Failures

Stephanie Paris

Consultants

Timothy Rasinski, Ph.D.
Kent State University

Lori Oczkus
Literacy Consultant

Matt Heverly
NASA Engineer

Based on writing from
TIME For Kids. TIME For Kids and the *TIME For Kids* logo are registered trademarks of TIME Inc. Used under license.

Publishing Credits

Dona Herweck Rice, *Editor-in-Chief*
Lee Aucoin, *Creative Director*
Jamey Acosta, *Senior Editor*
Lexa Hoang, *Designer*
Stephanie Reid, *Photo Editor*
Rane Anderson, *Contributing Author*
Rachelle Cracchiolo, *M.S.Ed., Publisher*

Teacher Created Materials

5301 Oceanus Drive
Huntington Beach, CA 92649-1030
http://www.tcmpub.com
ISBN 978-1-4333-4869-3
© 2013 Teacher Created Materials, Inc.

Table of Contents

Invention

New ideas lead to new inventions. Most items we use each day were invented by humans. Long ago, someone saw a need for a chair so they made one. Today, someone may see a way to make a new app, or perhaps there is an easier way to do something, like taking a bath. **Technology** includes electronics, such as computers or cell phones, but it also includes things as simple as a wheel or a needle. In any form, technology is designed to make our lives easier or more enjoyable.

Most inventions are easy to miss. They are small changes. If someone invents a new kind of wheel for skateboards, who will know? Pro skateboarders will be thrilled, and their fans will see the difference. But most of the world will never know anything has changed.

Sometimes, someone invents something that changes the world. What would life be like without phones or electricity? But not every invention is a success. For every new **feat**, there is at least one big failure.

- How is new technology developed?
- Why are failures and mistakes a big part of success?
- How have advances in science, technology, and engineering improved our lives?

Health and Survival

Video games and books make our lives more fun. Some inventions, such as paper clips and cars, make life easier. Other technology improves our chances of survival. Medical and health advances make people healthier. They fight diseases and ease pain. They help people live longer. And the longer we live, the more time we have to invent new things!

Fascinating Feat

The invention of the X-ray machine allowed doctors to see inside our bodies without cutting into them.

Hazards in the Home

Over 300 million people worldwide suffer from **asthma**. It's a condition that can make it hard to breathe. People with asthma have strong reactions to mold. But over time, we have perfected the chemical recipe for cleaning solutions. Someone invented a cleaning solution that kills mold and keeps it from growing in our homes.

A Royal Flush

As long as there have been people, there has been human waste. In ancient times, people buried it in a hole, but when they moved into cities, there wasn't room. New technology was needed.

In 1596, Sir John Harington invented a toilet that flushed. It thrilled Queen Elizabeth I. But it wasn't until 200 years later that flush toilets were used everywhere.

Sir John Harington

The Low-Flow

Toilets from before 1990 use more than 3.5 gallons of water with every flush. But newer low-flow toilets use 1.6 gallons of water with each flush. That saves over 11,000 gallons of water per household per year.

Watch Out Below!

Before we had toilets, people tried many different ways to get rid of waste.

In the past, people in cities used **chamber pots**. People liked that they could use them in the comfort of their own rooms. But what did they do when the chamber pot was full? They threw the contents out the window, and hopefully no one was standing below!

Outhouses took waste outside. But a walk to the bathroom in the middle of the night could be cold and dark.

The ancient Romans had public toilets. They built a long bench with holes in it over a deep trench with running water. People sat and chatted while they did their business!

Mold Juice

Many medicines save lives, but one of the most important medical inventions was an accident. In 1928, Alexander Fleming was working with **bacteria**. He knew many deadly diseases were caused by bacteria. One day, he looked at his samples. A mold **spore** had landed in the dish. The bacteria near the mold were dead. Fleming started working with the penicillium mold. He found it could kill many types of bacteria. At first, he called this substance *mold juice*. But soon he changed the name to *penicillin*. Penicillin was the first modern **antibiotic**. It was able to treat many infections. So many lives have been saved by the medicine, that it has been called a *miracle drug*.

antibiotics

Blood Bath

Doctors didn't always know what caused infections. For many years, doctors thought people could be cured by putting hungry leeches on them. Leeches are slug-like animals that drink blood. Unfortunately, this only made sick people weaker. Sometimes, it would even kill them.

Medical Meltdown

Some infections are caused by viruses, which are smaller and more dangerous than bacteria. Taking antibiotics for a viral infection won't help. In fact, it may hurt. If you take antibiotics too often, the bacteria will grow stronger and the antibiotics won't work when there's a bacterial infection.

E.coli bacteria

Frozen Foods

In 1912, Clarence Birdseye was in Canada. There, the Inuit (IN-oo-it) people showed him how to ice fish in very cold areas. The fish froze almost as soon as they were pulled from the water. When the fish were thawed and cooked, they tasted great! Birdseye went back to the United States. He now knew the secret to making delicious frozen foods. The faster the food froze, the better it would taste.

Clarence Birdseye

In 1925, he unveiled his Quick Freeze Machine. Other people had made frozen foods, but they weren't very good. Foods frozen in the new machine were much better. Soon, frozen foods were being sold in markets all over the world.

Quick Conversions

On the Fahrenheit scale, 32°F is the freezing point of water. The United States is one of the few countries that uses the Fahrenheit scale to measure temperature. Most of the world uses the Celsius scale. The following formulas show how to convert Celsius to Fahrenheit and Fahrenheit to Celsius.

Freezing point of water:
Fahrenheit 32°
Celsius 0°

Boiling point of water:
Fahrenheit 212°
Celsius 100°

Scientists believe food that is kept at 0°F will stay safe to eat forever. But most foods won't taste good forever!

Productivity

Clothes can be washed in a machine. Or they can be washed by hand. Either way, the clothes will be clean. But one takes a lot less work than the other. Hand washing takes a lot of effort. In a washing machine, many clothes can be cleaned at the same time. Throw in a load, add the soap, and press a button. This kind of technology improves **productivity**. That means the same work can be done without as much effort.

Electric Lights

Many inventors wanted to create electric lightbulbs. But none of them could make bulbs that lasted long enough. A team led by Thomas Edison finally did it. They found that cotton fibers baked into carbon glowed for 13 hours. A little later, they tried carbon made from bamboo. It lasted 1,200 hours!

Limitless Light

A lightbulb in Livermore, California, continues to burn after 110 years. It was first installed in 1901 to help the local fire department.

early lightbulb designs

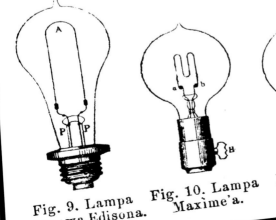

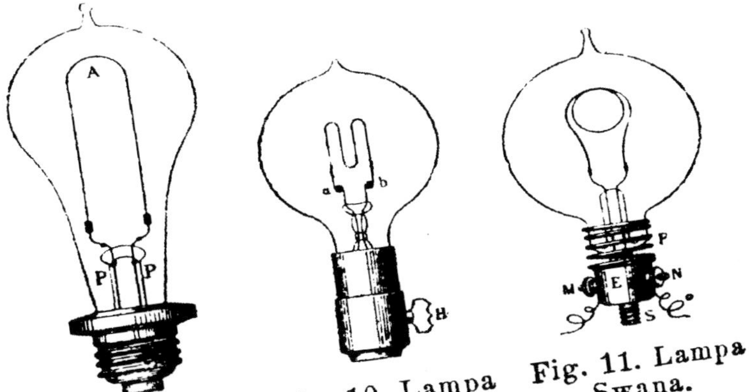

Fig. 9. Lampa żarowa Edisona.

Fig. 10. Lampa Maxime'a.

Fig. 11. Lampa Swana.

A Lightbulb Moment

Lightbulbs are everywhere—in your home, on the street, inside cars, even in the International Space Station. They are all around you, but have you ever taken a close look at what's inside one?

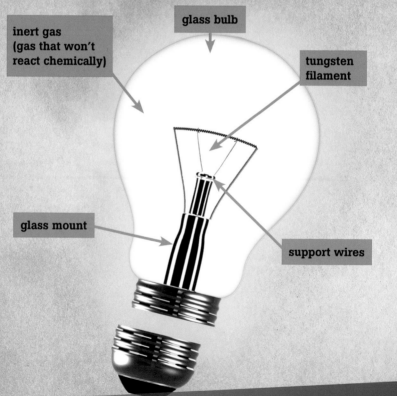

inert gas (gas that won't react chemically)

glass bulb

tungsten filament

glass mount

support wires

Only 10 percent of the energy in a regular lightbulb goes to make visible light. The other 90 percent makes heat!

Try Again!

Edison's team tried over 6,000 materials before they found the right one to make a long-lasting lightbulb. But Edison believed that every attempt taught them something new. He famously remarked, "I have not failed; I have just found 10,000 things that won't work!"

Lighting Facts per bulb

Brightness	**870 lumens**
Estimated Yearly Energy Cost	**$1.57**
Based on 3 hrs/day, 11¢/kWh	
Cost depends on rates and use	
Life	
Based on 3 hrs/day	**5.5 years**

Light

Warm — Cool

Energy Used	**13 watts**

Contains Mercury
For more on cleanup and safe disposal, visit epa.gov/cfl

Lightbulb packaging includes information about how much light each bulb produces.

Thomas Edison

Energy Sources

Before the lightbulb, people lit their homes with oil lamps. In the cities, natural gas lines were connected to houses. This let them use gas lamps. But they weren't very bright.

Thomas Edison knew he wouldn't sell many lightbulbs unless people had electricity in their homes. So he invented a system to get it to them. It was an important step in making electricity more popular.

Current Clash

Nikola Tesla thought alternating current (AC) was the best kind of electricity for people. Edison thought direct current (DC) was better. People debated which form was cheaper and which kind was safer. In the end, it was Tesla's AC idea that won out. Today, almost all the electricity we use is AC.

Nikola Tesla

Feat or Failure?

Sometimes, inventions and failures come together. For example, **fossil fuels** are **efficient** to use. And they are easy to transport. They opened the way for amazing new technologies like cars and airplanes. But they also pollute the environment. Now, scientists are working on ways to replace them.

Computers

In 1821, Charles Babbage had an idea. He wanted to make a machine that could **calculate**. In fact, he designed three. They were huge and too complicated for anyone to build them. But his ideas got things rolling. These machines would be the basis for future computers.

Charles Babbage

In 1976, two friends named Steve Wozniak and Steve Jobs had a different idea. They wanted to make smaller computers that anyone could use. Wozniak knew **microprocessors** were the key. They were small and inexpensive. In 1977, the friends started selling the Apple II computer. It was the start of the **Computer Revolution**.

Jobs and Wozniak working on Apple II

Ahead of His Time

During his life, people could see that Babbage's ideas were brilliant. But Babbage considered them failures because his machines were too complicated to build then. Later, engineers did build his machines. And they worked! Sadly, Babbage wasn't around to see it.

Babbage got his idea to use punch cards in his machine from this type of fabric loom.

First Programmer

The first computer program was written by Ada Byron, the Countess of Lovelace. She was a friend of Charles Babbage.

Then and Now

Can you imagine life without computers? Before them, work took more time. We didn't get as much done. And many things were impossible. Then computers came along. The earliest computers took up an entire room. They performed much simpler tasks than modern computers do.

The Electronic Numerical Integrator and Computer (ENIAC) was the world's first general purpose computer.

THEN

This 30-ton machine filled an entire room.

Workers were responsible for turning over 6,000 switches on and off.

It could multiply 5,000 numbers in a second. That was 1,000 times faster than a mechanical calculator. It could only run one program at a time.

The ENIAC was built in the United States in 1946.

Today, computers come in all different shapes and sizes. There are desktop computers, laptops, and tablets. And many things we don't think of as computers actually have computers inside them, such as cars and phones.

NOW

Modern computers are more than 100,000 times faster than the ENIAC.

Today's average computer weighs about 30 pounds. Laptop computers can weigh less than two pounds.

Tomorrow's computers may be as thin and flexible as a sheet of paper.

Communication

What is the most important invention? Many people say it's the printing press. At first, it may not seem special. But books and newspapers help people **communicate** with people near and far. Words and images help us trade information and ideas. We can learn about our best friend's new dog. Or we can tell people about a tiny new clock from Japan. The invention of the printing press lets us share our ideas with the world. Today, we share ideas through social media, email, television, and phones. People are always working on new ways to communicate. That's because there is always more to say!

"One should never underestimate the power of books."

—Paul Auster, writer

Printing Press

Today, the printed word is everywhere. Libraries are full of books. We can type something into a computer and send it out for thousands of people to read. But this wasn't always the case. Johannes Gutenberg (yoh-HAH-nes GOO-ten-burg) invented the movable-type printing press in 1440. Before that, books were hard to make. They had to be written and copied by hand. Only the rich were able to buy books. Most people didn't even know how to read. With the printing press, large quantities of books could be made easily and efficiently.

The Gutenberg Bible

The first major book printed using the press was the Bible. Today, only 21 complete copies remain. They are each known as Gutenberg Bibles. These are probably the most valuable books in the world. One volume sold for over five million dollars. And a single page may sell for up to $25,000!

Financial Flop!

The printing press was a huge success. But Gutenberg didn't become rich or famous in his time. His business partner sued him and gained control of his press. At one point, Gutenberg got into an argument with two archbishops and was **exiled** from the Catholic Church!

Gutenberg invented new oil-based ink for his printing press.

Cameras

Hundreds of years ago, cameras didn't exist. The only way to make a picture of a friend was to paint it. But in 1816, a man named Joseph Nicéphore Niépce (ZHOH-sef NEE-seh-fohr nee-EPS) had an idea. He started experimenting. By 1827, he had taken the world's first permanent photographs. They were black and white. And the subject had to stay still in front of the camera for eight hours!

Joseph Nicéphore Niépce

In 1888, George Eastman invented a new kind of **film**. It was flexible and easy to carry. Eastman made a simple camera to go with it. He called it the Kodak. With this film and camera, anyone could take pictures. It wasn't long before color photographs were invented. Then came motion pictures. Today, anyone can carry a camera and make movies in living color.

First Look

This is the oldest known photo taken by Niépce in 1825. It does not show a man and a horse. It shows an **engraving** of a man and a horse. Living things would have had to stay still for hours!

Movie Misfire!

Movies surround people with rich sights and sounds. Why not add in our other senses? In 1959, theaters tried letting people smell what was on the screen. A movie called *Scent of Mystery* was released. When certain pictures came on the screen, smells were pumped into the room. But the smells didn't reach people at the right time. Some people might have smelled grapes while a smoking pipe was on the screen!

Today, it's possible to take a digital photo and print it in seconds or send it to friends.

Telephone

Alexander Graham Bell's mother was deaf. So young Bell was fascinated by sound. He wanted to learn how sound travels. He thought if he changed sounds into electricity, he could send them across wires. He hired Thomas Watson, an electrical engineer. The two of them worked from Bell's ideas. They built a mouthpiece and an earpiece. They were connected by wire. It carried words spoken into the mouthpiece to the earpiece.

Bell called Watson from the other room. "Mr. Watson, come here. I want to see you!" These were the first words spoken across the wire.

"If you want to succeed, double your failure rate."

—Thomas Watson

Alexander Graham Bell

Billion-Dollar Bungle!

In 1998, a company called *Iridium* had a bold idea. It wanted people to be able to call from anywhere in the world. Unfortunately, the idea was extremely expensive! Plus, it required people to carry phones the size of bricks. Iridium lost over $1 billion dollars in its first six months.

Cell Phones Soar

Today, most Americans have cell phones. In fact, some *only* use cell phones. See how home-telephone use has declined while cell-phone use has risen by studying the average amount paid for these services over time.

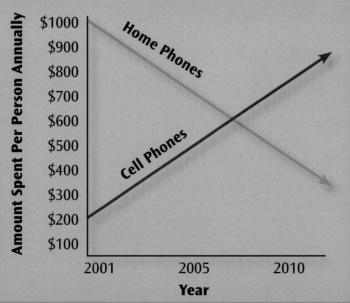

Eureka!

Did you just think of the world's next great gadget? Follow these steps to go from idea to invention.

① Imagine It!

Ask yourself what kind of invention would make life easier. Gather supplies and start brainstorming.

② Try It!

Build a sample and try it. Could it replace an older tool? Think about who might want to buy it and where you could sell it.

> "To invent, you need a good imagination and a pile of junk."
> —Thomas Edison

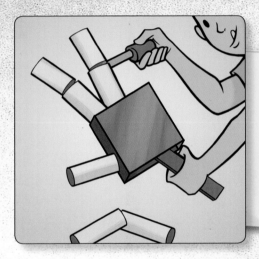

❸ Perfect It!

Make changes based on your test results. Bring in other experts to help, if needed.

❹ Patent It!

When your product is ready, take it to a **patent** lawyer. Filing a patent will protect your work from those who might want to take credit for it. Now, it's time to share it with the world!

Transportation

In prehistoric times, people walked. There were no cars, planes, or trains. Roads were simple dirt trails, flattened by the feet of humans and animals. Most people didn't go far from home. It could take an entire day to walk to the next village!

But as technology developed, the world became smaller. People could travel farther. The wheel was invented. Animals were used to help with work. In time, people put the two together. They made carts that could be pulled by animals. Traveling was becoming much easier. But it was only the start, and we are still exploring new ways to travel today.

Far Reaching

Advances in transportation don't move just people. Carts, trucks, trains, and planes ship food, mail, books, or clothes between places. Without these inventions, we would only be able to use the things that are right around us. And we could only know the people within walking distance of us.

Ramping Up

Ships
were used to explore the world for centuries. Today, they transport products between continents.

Horse and Buggy
carts were an early improvement over walking.

Trains
connected areas that were previously difficult to pass through.

Cars
allowed people to travel easily from the countryside into the city.

Airplanes
increased travel opportunities for everyone.

The Wheel

Today, the wheel seems like an obvious idea. But it didn't happen all at once. First, early humans used logs to roll heavy loads. These were called **rollers**. Next, they learned that putting **runners** under heavy things made them easier to drag. This was called a **sledge**. After that, they started to combine the sledge and the rollers. Soon, they noticed the sledge dug grooves in the runners. The grooves let the sledge move farther and faster. So they carved down the inner part of the rollers to make an **axle**. Pegs held the load in place, and the roller rolled underneath. The first cart on wheels was made!

Transport Trip-Up

The Segway is a kind of two-wheeled scooter. It was built so that it would be very difficult to fall down. It can go about 12.5 miles per hour. Faster than walking, but slower than biking, no one really knew what to do with it. By 2006, only about 24,000 had been sold.

Shaping the Wheel

The oldest wheel ever found was in Mesopotamia. It is probably about 5,500 years old. But researchers think the first wheels may have been made in Asia, around 8,000 BC. This diagram shows how early humans slowly learned to make wheels.

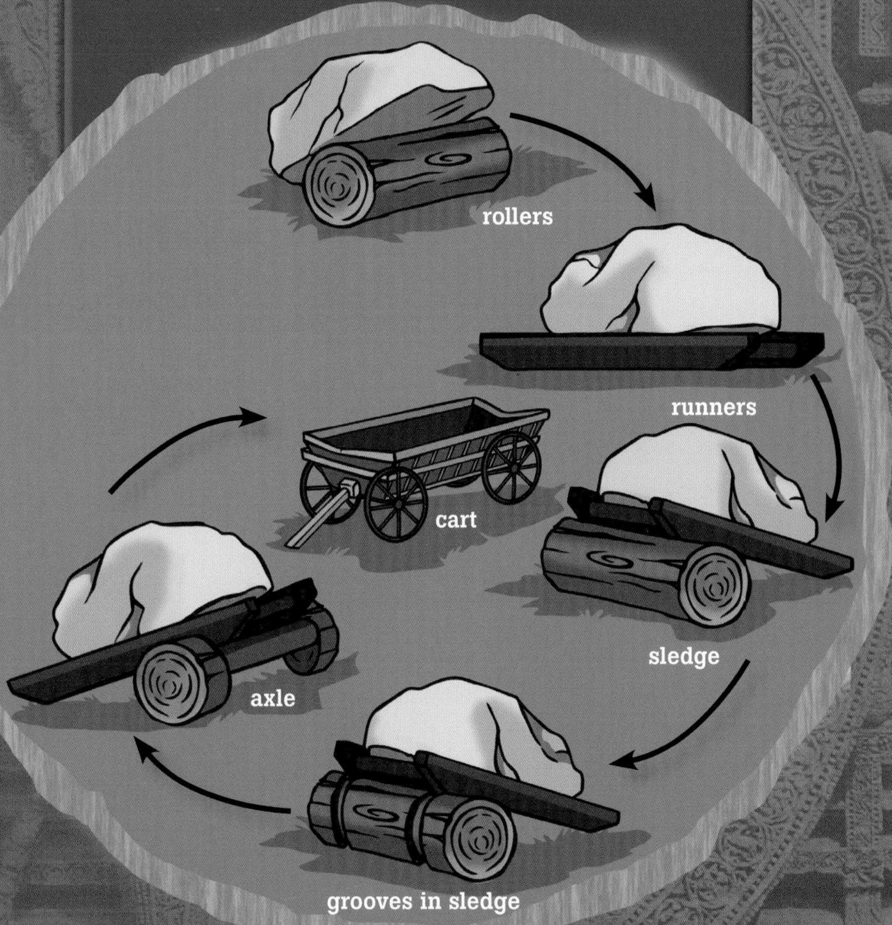

rollers

runners

cart

sledge

axle

grooves in sledge

Steam and Combustion Engines

Engines make things go. They allow us to travel great distances. In the 1700s, people learned how to run machines by heating water. Steam built up pressure. The pressure moved a pump. These pumps could be attached to all sorts of machines. They could run everything from factories to ships and trains.

During the 1800s, the **internal combustion engine** was created. In this engine, gasoline exploded in a small space. The explosion pushed up a piston. The force turned a wheel. Because the fuel was inside the engine, it was very efficient. It also meant the engines could be smaller—small enough to fit inside a car. As with so many inventions, the world hasn't been the same since.

High Hopes

In 1973, Henry Smolinski decided to make a car that could fly. He strapped the wings and tail from a *Cessna* airplane onto a Ford Pinto. Unfortunately, while he was testing it, the car broke free. The Pinto fell to Earth, killing the inventor and his passenger.

Parts and Pieces

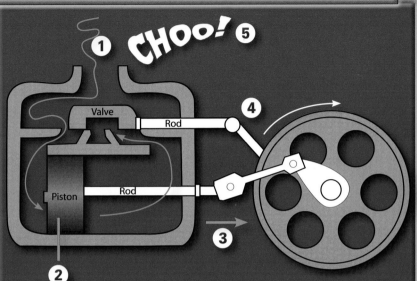

1 As water is boiled in a tank, it turns to steam. The pressure forces the steam into the engine.

2 As the steam builds up, it pushes the piston to the right.

3 The piston is attached by rods to the wheel. As the piston moves, it turns the wheel a half-turn.

4 As the wheel moves, the other arm slides a valve to the left. Steam then fills up the right side of the engine, pushing the piston left. This turns the wheel the rest of the way.

5 As the piston is pushed back and forth, it pushes the old steam, which is now exhaust, out of the engine. (This is where the "choo" sound comes from on a steam train.)

Highlights and Lowlights

Inventions have changed the world and will continue to do so for years to come. When they are first invented, it may be hard to tell a feat from a failure. But in time, true success is hard to miss!

800 BC

The flush toilet is invented in Ancient Crete, but the idea is lost until AD 1596.

AD 1842

Ada Byron writes the first computer program.

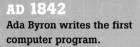

AD 1440

Johannes Gutenberg invents the printing press but makes little money from it.

STOP! THINK...

- Why do you think each of these inventions was important?

- What inventions do we still need today, and which ones are outdated?

- Why do you think there are so few women inventors listed on this time line?

AD 1928

Alexander Fleming discovers the power of penicillin—by accident.

AD 1976

Steve Jobs and Steve Wozniak invent the Apple II computer, which leads to thousands of new inventions.

AD 1959

Movies are a popular form of entertainment, but Smell-o-Vision stinks up theaters.

Glossary

antibiotic—a medicine that kills bacteria

asthma—a condition that causes difficulty breathing and tightness in the chest

axle—a pin, pole, or bar on or by which a wheel revolves

bacteria—one-celled organisms

calculate—to determine mathematically

chamber pots—bowls people kept in their rooms to collect human waste

communicate—to make known

Computer Revolution—a time beginning in the 1970s, when people began using smaller computers to do more tasks

efficient—capable of producing results without wasted time or energy

engraving—a print made using a metal or wooden plate with a design carved into it

exiled—to be kicked out or banished

feat—a great accomplishment

film—a thin roll or strip coated with a chemical sensitive to light and used in taking pictures

fossil fuels—the fuels made from plant and animal remains

internal combustion engine—an engine that produces power by burning fuel

microprocessors—tiny circuits that process information for computers

patent—a license that says you own the right to make an invention

productivity—the ability to get work done

rollers—cylinders that rotate around a central axis, for example, a rolling log

runners—strips of metal or wood placed under something to make it easier to drag

sledge—a sled for dragging heavy loads

spore—a small cell or reproductive part of bacteria or mold

technology—the use of knowledge to accomplish tasks, including machines, processes, and methods

Index

Bibliography

Chaline, Eric. *History's Worst Inventions.* **New Holland Publishers, Limited, 2009.**

Read about some of the world's worst inventions and their creators. There's the parachute overcoat, a locomotive too heavy for its tracks, and a test drug that nearly killed its test subjects!

Challoner, Jack. *1001 Inventions That Changed the World.* **Barron's Educational Series, 2009.**

This book includes photos and illustrations about the stories behind inventions in medical, electronic, transportation, and convenience items.

Claybourne, Anna. *The Story of Inventions.* **Usborne Publishing Limited, 2007.**

Find out about everything from the wheel to sticky notes, all with detailed illustrations. Learn how, when, and why many great inventions were made.

Daynes, Katie. *The Story of Toilets, Telephones and Other Useful Inventions.* **Usborne Publishing Limited, 2004.**

This book includes an amusing and informative history of the toilet, the telephone, frozen foods, soccer nets, space inventions, and more!

Frith, Alex. *See Inside Inventions.* **Usborne Publishing Limited, 2011.**

Flaps reveal detailed artwork showing the hidden workings inside inventions. The book also explains the differences among discovery, invention, and innovation.

More to Explore

How Stuff Works: Engineering Channel
http://www.howstuffworks.com

Click on the *Science* tab and then on the *Engineering* tab at the left. This website includes sections that describe how just about anything works, such as robots, water slides, and Segways.

Inventions and Technology Links
http://kids.nypl.org

Click on the *Science and Technology* tab in the top left corner. Click on the *Inventions and Technology* option to the right of the frog. This list contains multiple websites for inventions and technology.

Smithsonian Education: Students
http://airandspace.si.edu/wrightbrothers

Click on *Online Exhibition* to see an elaborate tribute to the Wright Brothers. The exhibit covers the invention of flying and includes some very rare photos of the Wright Brothers.

Time Specials: 50 Worst Inventions
http://www.time.com

Discover the best of the worst! In the search bar to the right, type *worst inventions*. Click on any of the *50 Worst Inventions* and navigate among them with the *Back* and *Next* buttons, or click on *View All* to see the list of all 50.

Kid Inventors in History
http://www.kidzworld.com/article/1010-kid-inventors-in-history

Learn about different inventions that kids have made throughout history. You may be surprised to learn what other kids have invented!

About the Author

Stephanie Paris is a seventh generation Californian. She has her BA in psychology from the University of California, Santa Cruz and her multiple-subject teaching credential from California State University, San Jose. She has been an elementary classroom teacher, a computer and technology teacher, a homeschooling mother, an educational activist, an educational author, a web designer, a blogger, and a Girl Scout Leader. She currently lives with her husband and children in Germany, where she loves checking out the latest gadgets and gizmos.